Journey Through

A

Living Testimony

"Thank God I woke up today, which means He has a purpose for my life! Now that I'm up, how can I empower somebody?"

By

Glenn A. Broom

N

NolatownPublishing
A Division of Nolatown Entertainment
2014

ISBN: 978-0-578-14692-8

Nolatown Publishing
New Orleans, Louisiana

Dedication

In the name of Jesus Christ, my personal savior, I'm truly blessed and highly favored and for that I give God all the praise and glory!!

To my wonderful parents who always believed in me, trusted me more than one can imagine and who prepared me for this world. My mother, Evelyn, taught me how to love unconditionally and that it's nice to be nice and my father Roland, taught me to be tough and to be a man. Thank God for blessing me with such a wonderful father. Rest in peace daddy, your job here is well done. Lord knows I miss you, so many cherished memories, but my faith assures me that you are in a better place and the Joy I feel in my heart because I know one day I will see you again. I love and honor you daddy and thank you for passing on the entrepreneurial trait.

To my wife, Erica, the true love of my life, the mother of my two wonderful children, my spouse, my confidant, my best friend, my Godmate and the queen of my castle standing with me at the throne of what all God has promised and my children, Kherron and Glenn Jr. who sacrificed, but endured and in spite of all the trials and tribulations, managed to pour their love and support into me.

To my brother Terrell, my sisters Carmen and Janice, my nephews and nieces, my Godparents, my In-Laws, my Godbrothers and Godsisters, my relatives, my friends, Berean Christian Church, my partners Rickey Spearman and Kemic Smothers and to all the angels and Godfriends without whom this book and all it represents would not have been possible.

To God Be The Glory!!!

Table of Contents

FOREWORD

"No weapon formed against the brothers of Nolatown shall prosper. You can tell the value of the man by the obstacles he has overcome to get to the present. That justifies his worth. No person has been as tried and prepared as us by the ups and downs of life. And within those adverse experiences lies the purifying power to bring life to the Seeds of Divinity within us. Whatever was meant by Satan for bad to us, God used it for good."

"By the world's standard and expectations, we don't belong here meaning we escaped from the traps Satan has set for our downfall. However, he is not the arranger or author of affairs. The Author of Time is in our favor for us to prosper because the predictions of old must be fulfilled. The meek shall inherit the Earth; the tail shall become the head. We are in the course of this now. The universe has a great abundance stored up for us in this day!!"

God Bless you,

Rickey Spearman
President & CEO, Nolatown

"If you do what you can, I'll do what you can't"

GOD

Introduction

This book represents an inspirational journey of divine reflection and expression from my deepest thoughts through a transformational spiritual insight, encounters and experiences with a strong unwavering belief that God works for the good of those who love Him, who have been called and when we have nothing left but God, God is enough!

I hope to convey through this book a strong message of what God has done in my life and if you trust in Him and take Him serious, He will come to your rescue! I wish to convey a sense of hope to those who have lost it and pray it helps somebody understand that even when the odds are against you, there is a way out of no way and through God the impossible becomes possible. Open your heart, clear your mind and humble yourself to receive the message that God is sending!

Bringing to mind PSALM 121, one of my favorite scriptures that I always turn to when things get complicated or the enemy attempts to deceive me, "I look up to the mountains - Where does my help come from? My help comes from the LORD, who made the heavens and the earth. He will not let you stumble or fall; the one who watches over you will not sleep. Indeed, he who watches over Israel will neither slumber nor sleep. The LORD himself watches over you! The Lord stands beside you as your protective shade. The sun will not harm you by day, nor the moon by night. The LORD will keep you from all harm and preserves your life. The LORD keeps watch over you as you come and go, both now and forever!"

Lastly, this notion of a book initially was an email that turned into a book and is the answer to the "why and how" questions from my family, friends and for those who "just couldn't see how I do it." I realize now that sometimes the journey is more important than the destination and through this book and compilation of thoughts, as well as quotes from those who inspire me, I hope that the reader is just as inspired and faithful after reading this book as I was in writing it. God has been so good to me and I simply refuse to let the enemy win! Thank God for blessing me with an ability of having such a way with words that it helps others, thus blessing me with the Grace to write!!

"And know that I am with you always; yes, to the end of time"

Jesus Christ

Katrina

August 30, 2005, "Tuesday morning following the storm, the city of New Orleans seemed to again have dodged a hurricane bullet, but then the levees gave way and the water started coming!"

"In one day, Hurricane Katrina wiped out two years of planning. In one day, I lost my plans, I lost my building, I lost my blueprints, I lost my income and I lost my market. I never realized firsthand water could do so much damage. There were places and streets that I had just traveled days before that were completely underwater, it was so surreal.

Two years prior to the storm I was commuting back and forth between New Orleans and Atlanta in a dual residency-type capacity. Therefore, the storm didn't affect me as much personally as it did businesswise. In fact, I was pretty much doing 100% business in New Orleans and at the time of the storm had some lucrative business deals transpiring, which included being part of the Virtual Office Suites out in New Orleans East, a Nolatown deal to acquire a historic downtown theater, as well my own building in Treme that I was redeveloping.

If you were a family member living anywhere outside of New Orleans, chances are you took in residents from New Orleans. We took in my wife's family, so it was fourteen of us and two dogs in our 3-bedroom townhouse in Georgia.

The stories are endless and I'm sure there are many future authors out there with stories to tell about Katrina. In my opinion, one of the worst losses, second only to the loss of life, was the lost of personal memories and the mementos that have no replacement value!!"

Reflective Perspective –Glenn A. Broom, author

"I see a city within a city, there's a white wall around it, that wall is to keep the enemy out, because this is something that God is building. I'm here to tell you that, Lincoln Beach is already done. So, no matter what difficulties or obstacles you are experiencing now, it doesn't matter because this is already done."

"Pursue, Overtake and Conquer!!"

Minister-Prophet Barbara Clewis

GodFriend

The sweetness of a friend's counsel that comes from the heart rejoices the heart. I've learned in this journey of life that there are three seasons that God brings special people into your life, Event, Era or Eternity. Sometimes we depend on our own understanding and we want to bring them in the season we want them in. I think everyone that comes into your life is not always there because they had a purpose in your life, maybe you were a purpose in theirs. I call these divine links, "Godfriends," those unforeseen connections that keep the blessings forever moving to simply prove that God is!

A "Godfriend" is a friendship where you find kindness, understanding and support! A friendship in the heart that physically doesn't end until the heart stops and spiritually never ends! Indeed a friendship when the need arises that can pick-up the conversation from wherever it ended last and never a feeling too burdensome to call on! A friendship that is thoughtful and knows what to say, knows when to say it and knows what not to say where a misunderstanding is resolved with an agreement to disagree! A silly friendship that makes sadness smile and at the same time have you crying from laughter where pride takes a backseat to humility! A kindred friendship that knows when to be serious that would record your praises in front of you and sing your praises behind your back! A fellowship confidant that can lift you up in prayer, lift you up in Word or simply just lift you up! An unselfish ally who is confident within themselves that sees you for who you are and not being judgmental thus sparing you the cosmetic significance where the boundaries of criticism are only positive! A candid friendship where what you need to hear outweighs what you want to hear and corporate charades of the world are not required! A meaningful friendship where integrity, morals, values and love are never compromised thus being faithfully responsible within their own independence!

I love you Godfriend and what a friend we have in Jesus!!

"We the willing, led by the unknowing, are doing the impossible for the ungrateful. We have done so much, with so little, for so long, we are now qualified to do anything, with nothing."

Mother Teresa

Help is Coming

Drowning on dry land, but my faith assures me that I won't drown. Therefore, I'm not worrying about anything and I'm praying about everything. I've told God what I need and I thank Him for all He has done! What I have witnessed has taught me to trust God for what I haven't witnessed and not to depend on my own understanding!

I had a talk with God and when I shared what we talked about, I was told to stop dreaming and come back to reality. Isn't it amazing that people pray and ask God to deliver and when he does, people don't believe it or recognize it?

If they understood my relationship with God then they wouldn't think my faith is blind, but at the same time if I could see it, then it wouldn't be faith. I trust God because God has shown me time after time that He can be trusted. They don't understand that I do it from a position of fear based on all the knowledge I have of God. God don't play and when I started taking Him serious He came to my rescue. Therefore, I will continue to do God's will, spread the Word and they will never, ever understand my glory if they don't understand my story!

I will not allow my integrity to God to be questioned nor will I question God. The devil is a liar and I choose to use my gift of free will to live in a way pleasing to God. I realize now that Life is the precious commodity in this world ruled by the devil, and because Life is of God, the world under the devil's authority is full of hatred, deceit, cruelty and greed. In a world under the guidance of such a misleading force, where most of us rely on our own human understanding, it's no wonder there is so much suffering!

Prophesying with edification in this world of ongoing spiritual warfare, God is not the cause of suffering, the devil is! In this misguided world where sinful humans fight for control which leads to crimes, wars and oppression and unforeseen events that lead to more suffering, it's comforting to know that I have God as a father and Jesus as a brother!

It comes a time in this world when we all need help. Before one can conquer this world, he or she must first be saved from it! I'm faithful enough to know that it is in my weakness where God provides strength, wise enough to know that Jesus is the supplement and humble enough to know that strength is not determined by the amount of weight that can be lifted, but by the amount of weight through faith, God's grace and mercy you can hold up!

The constant in this ever changing world is God, and Jesus is the path to salvation and He has conquered the world. Therefore, don't despair, be encouraged, and stay faithful because help is coming!!

Enemy's House Warming

April 9, 2007, "A week before, we were blessed with a new house built from the ground with nothing and in our joy, still trying to figure out how we qualified. The joy was short-lived; and before we could set-up anything, our home was burglarized a week later. I would have been home, but my wife had an appointment downtown and asked me to go along. The robbers broke in through a glass door they shattered at the rear of the house, opened the garage door, backed their car in and cleaned us out. Thank God we were out, thank God they didn't harm Sweetpea, our pet schnauzer and thank God we qualified!!"

Reflective Perspective –Glenn A. Broom, author

"The test of adversity is one that's fought with faith."

Drew Brees

My Role, My Purpose and The Difference a Day Makes

I understand your role, but you don't understand mine and you don't understand your role as it relates to me. Understanding my glory requires that you know my story. Therefore, don't conclude until the entire story is read. Slow down on the highway to the intangibles and the so called reality shows of the world, weaving through the traffic jam of your own understanding, classified in the middle from assets shrouded in liabilities to the limited results of the rat race or you will divinely bypass Thee miracles!

Prevalent in this world today is the bargaining with God, while paying the world in full and the fear of God nearly nonexistent. God is always having to prove Himself because many of us pray for answers but don't sit still long enough to receive them or too busy to realize that He comes to us in many signs, ways and forms, but many only would acknowledge God's presence nothing short of a burning bush! Therefore, blinded by pride and taking the miracles that happen every day for granted. The reality is that we are in spiritual warfare caught up in this wilderness of a matrix we call the World and as the battle lines are being drawn, many are asleep, moving aimlessly and robotically through this God-given phenomenal opportunity we call Life! We all have a role, a purpose in God's kingdom, and when you understand what that is, you produce!

It took me some years to realize, but in one day I gained a keen understanding, a spiritual insight with a Corinthians' love and a divine trust I never experienced before. Allowing my spirituality in a human experience to determine my reality, in one day, a projectory in my life that had it not been for this transformational journey and the sacrifices, then I wouldn't have relied on God or known how faithful, powerful and resilient I've become. Faithfully knowing that no matter how hard the pitch or the curve the world throws at me, I've humbled myself to be the hit that God intended for me to be with a glorious appreciation and a deep adoration for family and friends; fully understanding it's Love that makes a house a home, not possessions!

Studying the Word that allows me to stay a step ahead of the enemy, I recognize that God's Will won't ever take you where God's Grace won't see you through and the difference a day makes is a day of understanding and knowing Jesus is worth a lifetime of not knowing Him!

Corinthians tells us, "brothers and sisters, God chose us to be His. Not many of us were wise in the way the world judges wisdom. Not many of us had great influence, and not many of us came from important families. But God chose the foolish things of the world to shame the wise. He chose the weak things of the world to shame the strong. And God chose what the world thinks is not important—what the world hates and thinks is nothing. God chose things to contest what the world thinks is important." In short, He chose the best in us!

Clocked out the pride and clocked in the humility while raising up the praises with testimony in overtime! Most never quite understand the value of planning nor do they acknowledge the effort that goes into it. I'm mindful of God's timing and know the difference in being patience with a plan that comes with vision, passion and purpose, from foolishness in having no plan and waiting without vision, passion and purpose! No longer will I fall into the same traps and be hoodwinked, bamboozled, led astray or run amok!

I've learned to deal with the things I can control and not waste time on things I cannot. In a place where my value is perceived as less, I'll continue to work twice as hard; I'll continue to teach my children to love, not to hate and to recognize the enemy by the content of their character, not by the color of their skin. I'll continue to show them that a plan, patience, humility, persistence and faith are the ingredients for success. I'll continue to empower others and build my value before God whose perception is the only one that I'm truly concerned about!

For I have finally figured it out that the devil always attacks my weaknesses and God uses my strengths. God chose the best in me and I will use the favor that has been bestowed upon me in a way that is pleasing to God and a detriment to the plan of the enemy!

Thank God for blessing me with an innate ability for process, an understanding of how the numbers work in regards to the process and the ability to translate this information to paper. Thank God I woke up today, which means He has a purpose for my life! Now that I'm up, how can I empower somebody?

Living in the Spirit

Thy kingdom come let it be written and let His will be done! In my transformational journey, I'm a modern day disciple in God's new army spreading the Word and love of Jesus Christ my Savior, living physically in this world called reality, yet independent of it. With the praying love of my family, God as my pilot and Jesus as my navigator, I rise above to a higher place of consciousness to truly live in Spirituality!

Therefore, I'm seeking a fundamental shift toward the principles of Jesus Christ in every way, including complete devotion to God and as I grow into this discipleship, which as Jesus told me would be accompanied by hardships and difficult times filled with times of trials and tribulations along with times of blessing. I humbly ask the Lord to continue allowing an anointing spirit to move in my life, to be a beacon to empower others and to have an uncluttered serving heart! As my understanding becomes clearer and I can now recognize the attacks of the enemy, it's again comforting to know that I have God as a father and Jesus as a brother!

Consequently, my heart finds comfort and my mind at ease knowing the words of Jesus, I digest the bread of Jesus and He is in me as He is in God!!

"When you know who you are, people can't make you what they want you to be."

Pastor Kerwin B. Lee

My Testimony (February 13, 2011)

"First of all, I would like to thank Pastor Lee for all that he does and to our family here at Berean Christian Church for allowing me to share my testimony. My name is Glenn Broom and a couple of weeks ago my son was involved in the incident many of you I'm sure heard about through the media involving the mother who pick up the teens from school and proceeded to rob a bank which ended in a high speed police chase and crash.

I'm so thankful I had God in my life; otherwise it would have been impossible for me to get through let alone to be the strength for the rest of my family. I'm also thankful for his attorney, Stacy Levy and all the support and prayers from family and friends.

Prior to the hearing, I spoke with several attorneys who informed me that the chances of the charges, of this serious nature, being dismissed during the probable cause hearing were slim to none and how the window for the burden of proof was so small for the prosecution. What they didn't know is the God I serve and believe in is the Master of Probability. Justice prevailed, the robbery charges were dropped and my son was released.

We will continue to pray for the other teens, the mother and their families in this unfortunate life-changing ordeal. The devil is a liar, JESUS loves me and GOD continues to be good all the time!! Thank God my son is alive and has been given a chance to tell his side and to clear his name! In Jesus name I pray, Amen!!!"

Reflective Perspective –Glenn A. Broom, author

"It's easier to build strong children than to fix broken adults."

Frederick Douglas

Family's God Kind of Love

"The Brooms!"

A family that pray together, stay together, and even when the ones closest to you don't understand, lose hope or even lose faith, I've learned that there is no argument against "God" and at the end of the day, Love has to endure. Therefore, in a relationship, your Godly life will speak to them better than any words. They will be won over by watching your pure, Godly behavior!

Thank God for my family. You see we love each other with a God kind of love, and we dwell in peace. For me and my house will serve the Lord and I will not allow the enemy to break apart what God has joined together nor will I allow my Joy to be stolen at the benefit of the enemy! When God is for you, it doesn't matter who's against you. A family united stands while a divided family falls. God continue to bless my family with love and renewed faith!!

"We didn't have much, but we had love."

Tyler Perry

Lord, Take My Hand!!

It's rarely easy to make a life transition, but God this one seems especially difficult. I'm trying to be brave, but there is so much uncertainty and I lack the confidence to successfully adjust to my new situation.

Lord, please walk me through this change, step by step. Help me not to cling stubbornly to the past nor try looking too far into the future. Where my self-confidence ends, let my confidence in You begin. In Jesus name I pray, Amen!!

Beloved Wife,

Evelyn C. Broom

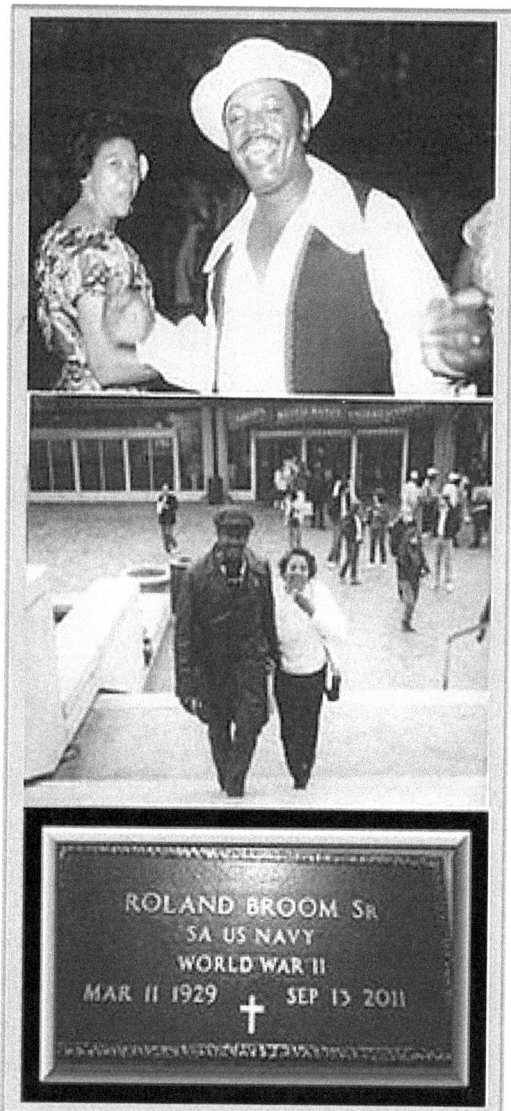

ROLAND BROOM Sr
SA US NAVY
WORLD WAR II
MAR 11 1929 ✝ SEP 13 2011

"If you don't like something, change it. If you can't change it, change your attitude."

Maya Angelou

NOLATOWN

Nolatown (hence the name) is to be for New Orleans, what Motown was for Detroit, a local vehicle with style and class that will draw national and international interest!!

If anyone had told me I was going to be a developer years earlier, I wouldn't have believed it because it wasn't in my plan. However, it was in God's plan and once you start working on a God's plan, the enemy gets busy and starts working on you!!

From: Sandra Brownlee
To: Glenn Broom @Nolatown
Subject: Re: Veterans Metro-Plex Overview

Date: Wed, 2 Oct 2013 11:02:39

"Thanks Glenn. It was a pleasure to meet with you on yesterday. On behalf of all Veterans, I would like to say thank you all for this amazing gesture of gratitude and patriotism. Thank you all so much."

--

Sandra Brownlee
MSGT/Retired Army

The Man I've Become

For I have been under great pressure, far beyond my ability to endure and left to my own understanding, I believed I was in despair even of what I knew to be the joys of life. For how great Jesus love towards me that He delivered me from bondage. God has set me free and it's through my love of Jesus Christ, I'm assured God releases any and all kinds of chains; be they physical, mental, financial, emotional, circumstantial or sinful!

Therefore, I will not allow my heart to be blocked, my mind to be cluttered or my faith to be compromised. On the contrary, my heart is open, my mind is free and studying the Word solidifies my faith. I know now that there is power in the spoken Word. Thus, I'm spreading the Word, God is real and Jesus is coming!

Had it not been for this journey and the sacrifices, then I wouldn't have relied on God or known how faithful, powerful and resilient I've become. I realize by God's Grace, I'm an imperfect humble man in a transformation of life, surrendering the wants of the flesh to get what the Spirit needs and no matter what I have endured; God has a purpose for my pain. It's through the pain that have made me into whom I've become; a better man, a better husband, a better father and a better friend. I now have clarity, mindful not to let my own desires become bigger than God's agenda and no matter how hard the pitch or the curve the world throws at me, I'll continue being faithful, thus being the hit that God intended for me to be!

Don't focus on the man I was; focus on the man I've become. I've humbled myself to never be too proud to serve God, praise Him anywhere or to ask for help. I'm able to recognize help as a blessing; not a handout, to be grateful; not disappointed, to be forgiving; not angry and to know that in God's timing that I will be a blessing to empower others. I rather be disrespected, ridiculed and talked about serving God than respected serving the world!!

"If you don't stand for something you will fall for anything."

Malcolm X

Beautiful Day

May 31, 2014, "It's a beautiful day, I just walked a mile and a half in 86-degrees to access the Internet at the library; I'm hot, sweating and I get there and the computers are down and thieves have stolen the copper from HVAC units at the library, which means there's no AC. I turned around, it's a beautiful day, and walked a mile and a half back home; thank God I can walk!!"

Reflective Perspective –Glenn A. Broom, author

"The downs will make you appreciate the ups so don't ever get tired of doing the right thing, you must hit all the steps to success and God replaces manufactured fun with Joy!"

Steve Harvey

Queen

The connection has been made, for as woman came from man, subsequently a man is born of woman, independent of neither, but all from God! Therefore, I respect the power of a woman and I recognize that God is the only one that can neutralize that power. For you precious woman who has endured so much, I thank God for you!

With an understanding that there is no argument against God, I'll continue to show her my Godly life, my Godly behavior, and I'm again submitting myself to God to be all that He intended for me to be and I'm resisting the devil, therefore he will flee from me. For it is unconditional love that endures, even after faith and hope are misplaced!

Consequently, I'm loving in a Corinthians way and I've learned to cultivate her heart and thus her very Essence. In other words, the set of attributes that make a woman what she fundamentally is, and which she is by necessity, and without, loses her identity. In translation, all that God meant for her to be, a Queen!

Humbly I ask her to put her faith in God and trust me to do what God has placed in my heart. For how can I be an example for my Prince or produce and raise a Princess if I don't love, honor, respect and cherish my matrimonial Queen with whom I consummated these glorious blessings or my maternal Queen who produced and raised me?

For wisdom has graced me with an understanding that life experiences will humble youthful desires and I no longer fall into some of the same traps set by the enemy that I felled for in the past. I've learned to treat her anger with kindness, to match her intellect with wisdom, to stay out of the way of her monthly hormonal mood swings and to accept the fact that I will never fully understand her, but find solace in that she will never fully understand me!

At the end of the day, to find the humor to make her smile, thus finding the keyhole to her heart and if all else fails in my own limited understanding, I sacrificially pray making sure that we never fall out of love at the same time. For you are my Queen!!

"A wise woman knows the importance of speaking life into her man. If you love him; believe in him, encourage him and be his peace!"

Denzel Washington

GodMate

I met my wife, Erica at an international party that I was supposed to be taking another young lady to who cancelled on me at the last minute. What can I say; we clicked. I'll first date was a Luther Vandross (one of our favorites) concert if that is any indication of where this relationship was going!

What can I say about Erica in three words or less? She's a character! What can I say about marriage in seven words or less? It should not be entered into lightly! Would I do over again? Absolutely!

I have been with Erica over half of my life and the love I have for her is unconditional. After being together for 32 years, 26 of those years married and 2 wonderful children (blessings), I think I can speak on it!

I believe our matrimony journey is more than a milestone, a benchmark or even a midlife event, but simply a matured-divine understanding of "we as one" and what God has joined together, let no one put asunder!

I've read that "the loyalty of a woman is tested when a man has nothing and the loyalty of a man is tested when he has everything!"

Many nights I slept with one eye opened and at times, in my own limited understanding, not really knowing if it was love or obligation, but when it's all said and done, "I rather have bad times with Erica, than good times with someone else, I rather be beside Erica in a storm than safe and warm by myself, I rather have hard times together than to have easy apart, I rather have Erica, the one who truly holds my heart!"

I believe God put people in your life for a reason and that also includes the ones that you spent the rest of your life with. You know, until death do you part. Some may call it your soulmate, but I believe it's your Godmate!

Erica, the true love of my life, the mother of my two wonderful children, my wife, my confidant, my best friend, my Godmate and the queen of my castle standing with me at the throne of what all God has promised, I thank God for you!!

God has been so good to us and I give him all the praise and glory. According to Proverbs 12:4 and 6:18-19, "a worthy wife is her husband's joy and crown; a shameful wife saps his strength. Let your wife be a fountain of blessing for you and rejoice in the wife of your youth. She is the loving doe, a graceful deer. Let her breasts satisfy you always ("they still do") and may you always be captivated by her love" ("I still am")!

Happy Birthday

June 2, 2014, "I woke up thanking God and reflecting on the blessing He gave my wife and me 25 year ago, in this, a beautiful bundle of joy with dimples and later that night feeling like the enemy again challenging God by testing our faith and almost seeing our blessing taken away on the very day she came to be. I got the call from my daughter, who while out celebrating her birthday with her friends, was involved in an accident in her car that was hit in the rear by another car, side swiped in the front and knocked into ongoing traffic. It turned out to be a "Happy Birthday" after all; thank God for traveling Grace and thank God for hearing our daily prayers for covering our children!!"

Reflective Perspective –Glenn A. Broom, author

"God, grant me the Serenity to accept the things I cannot change,
the Courage to change the things I can,
and Wisdom to know the difference."

Reinhold Niebuhr

Credit Where Credit Is Due

God has declared individual promises to each of us and they will come according to His will. Just hold on, it will be fulfilled. Lord, you are God all by yourself! I honor and praise you, because you have done amazing things. You have always done what you said you would do; you have done what you planned long ago!

If it was easy, then I would personally take credit and think that I alone made it happen when in fact, it's not about me!! It's about the purpose that God has for my life and understanding that I have to seek God out in order to fulfill my purpose. Once that is accomplished, then giving the credit to God will help others and defeat the enemy!

I find it amazing that all that God does for us; He is forever having to prove Himself worthy. Like the Israelites, who forgot God departed the Red Sea allowing them to walk to freedom, only to end up back in bondage as a result of depending on their own understanding and to those who truly believe that it's an alarm clock that wakes them up in the morning, never give up because our spirits are being renewed every day. The enemy knows if he blocks and create doubt then God will never get the credit, praise and glory that are rightfully His!

Let me be worthy of God's grace and be a beacon to empower others. Clearly, no one has ever seen, no one has ever heard, and no one has ever imagined what God has prepared for those who love Him. But God has shown us these things through the Spirit!

So the Lord said to me, "Not by might nor by power, but by my Spirit!!" "Do all you can and I'll do all you can't," says the Lord Almighty. Therefore, enemy get off my back, I will not allow your burdens to weigh me down. You see, I'm living in the spirit of the Lord, spreading the word and as my praises are lifted in testimony, thank you Jesus, the credit; honor and glory all belong to you!!

"Someone's sitting in the shade today because someone planted a tree a long time ago."

Warren Buffett

House Is A Home
("Turned the key and my family was still there!")

For awhile now, I have been putting out fires with no water, but I'm sending the praises up and the blessings are raining down. Therefore, through God's grace and mercy, I'm allowing perseverance and patience to finish its work so that I may be mature and complete lacking nothing and no matter what I have endured, God has a purpose for my pain. I'll continue having a serving heart, showing them my Godly life, my Godly behavior and purposely existing while being cognizant of my spiritual requirements!

The most difficult part of this journey is the things that my family had to endure and the sacrifices that were made. Thank God for the love and teachings of my parents who prepared me, along with God's will and guidance that allowed me to rather than let these things tear my family a part, allowed me to keep my family intact? Although at times "they" questioned my mental capacity and my job taking skills or had doubts or lost hope or even lost faith, the one thing that kept us together is a Corinthians' love that we have for each other!

I realize it's one thing for me to go out so far of my comfort zone and quite another to take my family with me out of theirs. How could I lead by God if I never seriously followed Jesus or not live by the Word even though I considered myself a Christian? I'm abundantly blessed and shining in the favor that God has bestowed upon me. You see, once I realized that I couldn't serve two masters because two opposing forces cannot occupy the same vessel at the same time, I surrender all, took God serious and He came to my rescue! In my rescue, I focused on what God said and not what I or others saw. I overcame the fear of being absence from a physical world in order to be present in a spiritual one. Instead of being thankful for a man seeking a righteous spirit, they're praying for a man to seek a right job!

Hence, "I have a job" when I was recruited by Jesus and I started working for God, I stopped fearing the consequences of debt and was no longer a slave to it!

Out of bondage through God's Grace that has sustained me; I now clearly understand that money can't buy happiness, intelligence or love. With no pride to swallow because humility fills my mouth where unexplainable victories were snatched from the jaws of defeat, asking for help no longer felt like a handout, but a blessing. Humbled myself to be grateful; not disappointed and started counting the miracles, not the time. Allowing my spirituality to determine my reality and not complaining, I acknowledged the power of money and understand now that the power of God is greater. Completely recognizing that money only amplifies whatever the situation already is; thus, unconditional family love is blasting in my house!

For my house, built from the ground with nothing, is a home and by opening the door of my heart, allowing God in my home, I recognize now, for I who in this world has nothing has everything in Christ and by God's Mercy have done so much with so little for so long that I'm now humbly qualified to do anything with nothing. It's perfectly clear, to know that in God's timing that I will be a blessing to empower others by not allowing any doubt to destroy my faith. Silently carrying the burdens unbeknownst to my family, encouraging them not to conclude until the entire story is read. For it is in the balance I seek, the quality of life, not the quantity that determines the purpose for my life in order to achieve the divine harmony for which I was chosen!

Fully aware in the struggle that a family that prays together stays together, I thank God for my family. You see we love each other with a God kind of love, and we dwell in peace. For me and my house will serve the Lord and I will not allow the enemy to break apart what God has joined together. It was only through God's directions that guided me through the frustrations and the impatience of the gang of two black women and a young black man. No bitterness, no malice and no anger here. You see, for it was during these times when I needed a best friend, God sent TeddyB!

Thank God for family and friends and for the angels sent to fight the demons. Consequently as I pray, I rebuke the enemy, bypassing the traps of the past; being a promoter for God with a spiritual clarity to recognize the attacks of the enemy and boldly sounding the horn not allowing the ones closest to me to be consumed while singing a new hymn of praise to God with renewed faith!

Recognizing the blessing in the matrimonial laundry time or an angel sent as a court-appointed attorney or losing the upstairs AC to a power surge caused by a strike of lightning four months after the warranty expired or even ending up on an air mattress after losing our bed to bugs, I realize now that sometimes the journey is more important than the destination and fully understand that in the course of faith and persistence, it takes 30 years of hard work to become an overnight success!

When it's all said and done, my family is what truly matters and the greatest gift I can give is all of me. When I climbed the stairs of this journey and turned the key, my family was still there and still in love with me. Thus, my ultimate aspiration, fulfillment and gratitude are that as it happens for them it happens for me!

Thank God, the struggle is over!!

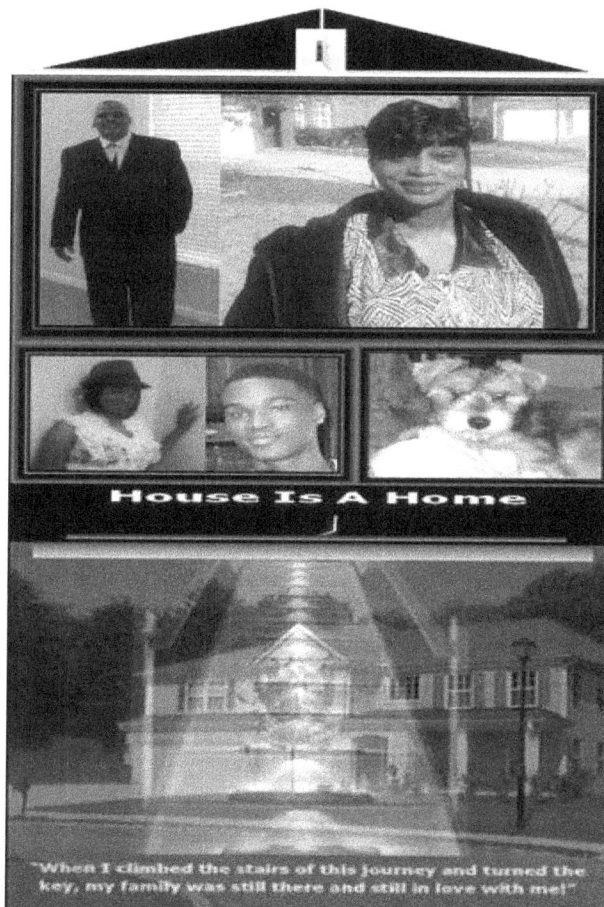

House Is A Home

"When I climbed the stairs of this journey and turned the key, my family was still there and still in love with me!"

"A good leader can engage in a debate frankly and thoroughly, knowing that at the end he and the other side must be closer, and thus emerge stronger. You don't have that idea when you are arrogant, superficial, and uninformed."

Nelson Mandela

Joy Inside My Tears

God's Favor & Grace that gives me Joy in
spite of what I'm going through!

Joy inside my tears!!

For me, being spiritual is helping others, working on the things I can control, praying for the things I can't and it's believing in something bigger than me. It's replacing fear with faith, doubt with assurance and stress with peace. It's doing all I can and trusting in God to do all I can't. It's having a serving heart and loving in a Corinthians way with no malice in my heart. It's professing the love I have for Jesus for being my savior, thus assuring my salvation. It's speaking as if it were; its faith and I've learned there is always a place for God. It's spreading the Word and giving all the praise, honor and glory to God. It's singing a hymn of praise with renewed faith. It's having Joy in spite of the trials and tribulations; it's fulfilling my purpose and being who God intended for me to be!

I'll continue to show my Godly life, my Godly behavior in spite of the recognizable attacks from the enemy because God is truly my source and for that reason, I've become a minister of my experiences, a promoter of God and a beacon to empower others!

Finally, it's moving with the favor that I believe I have with an absence of arrogance and a presence of humility to simply prove and glorifying that God is and it's being a soldier in this spiritual warfare with tears from that Joy I have in spite of what I'm going through!!

"It took a lot of blood, sweat and tears to get to where we are today, but we have just begun. Today we begin in earnest the work of making sure that the world we leave our children is just a little bit better than the one we inhabit today."

President Barack Obama

Use Me Up

The constant in this ever-changing journey is my loving faith in Jesus Christ, love of a family intact and the continued blessings from God. It was something in one of those Sunday sermons that made me take a look back at my past business successes and failures. Sometimes the devil is not always busy and sometimes God allows a wrench to be thrown into the plan when you take too much credit; become too worldly; get too arrogant or you're not humble enough. Let's just say, it brings you to your knees!

Quoting legendary boxer Joe Louis, "everybody wants to go to heaven, but nobody wants to die." For those that don't understand there is no "but" after God and believed that the sacrifice wasn't necessary or the time perceived as lost, is actually restored by the miracles that go unnoticed and the path faithfully travelled leads to the reason for purpose of the chosen path in the first place. How could you ever understand not having, if you never experienced the sacrifice of doing without or ever reach the humility that comes from that experience?

In all things, God works for the good of those who love Him and who have been called according to His purpose. The more I relied on God, the more it forced me to seek the truth in the Word and the more I sought the truth, the clearer my understanding, thus my purpose became. Before I could conquer the world, I first had to be saved from it! Therefore, surrendering to God's will and sacrificing what the world had to offer was a must and accepting anything less than 100% focused effort, ignoring the signs, the past experiences or the prophetic words of a stranger, would be conceding to the distractions of the world, and thus not reaching what all God intended for me to be!

Constantly saying to the ones that know and love me, especially my family, not to focus on the man I was and to focus on the man I've become. All in an attempt to convince them that I'm not crazy and it's me, but something is going on here beyond a human understanding! All the while showing them my Godly life, my Godly behavior in hope of conveying to them that my talks with God was not a dream and the reality is, finding a man with a righteous spirit is getting a man with a righteous heart! Finally, understanding that simply believing in God is not enough; I must also do His will and putting it all together by relating devotion, God's mercy and His promises in the Word, to following Jesus in my personal experience through this world and in my transformation, applied it to my life!

You see, it was times I had no money and no car, nor did I no longer follow the so-called standard employment path into the rat race, but I did have a self-employed plan with a PhD in patience, the love and support of family and friends, the protection of angels sent to fight the demons, the power of God that garners me respect, faith that earns me trust, blessed with wisdom to be able to teach and the love of Jesus that gives me strength, as well as, God's Grace that sustains me! Let it be written, let it be said, I belong to God and Jesus has guided the way! Therefore, devil there's nothing for you here, so flee, as my heart is beating to the Glory of the coming of the Lord! Furthermore, God is so good to me, "I wanna spread the news that if it feels this good being used, God just keep on using me…, until You use me up!"

My Lord, thank you for all that You do and for carrying me when I couldn't carry myself. Many Sundays when asked to raise your gifts to the Lord, I raised an empty hand. Thanks to you God, my hand isn't empty anymore. I'm humbly rejoicing on this day that the Lord has made and I'm grateful to be in it; for I am truly blessed and highly favored and for that I give God all the praise, honor and glory. The seeds have been planted long ago and my instructions in prophecy, to pursue, overtake and conquer, are clear. The business plan for this part of the journey is complete and I have a roadmap for the world. I understand it now, the devil may be the CEO of the world, but God is the Chairman of the Board and Jesus has successfully overcome the world!

So as I grow into this discipleship, being a minister of my experiences and my praises are lifted in testimony, I will shout from the mountaintops, the podiums, the pedestals and the platforms that God is my source, Jesus is the code and now, undeniable, undoubtable and unquestionable, it's time to work the plan!!

A Note to Myself

As God is my source; in Him will I trust: He is my shield, and Jesus is the bridge to my salvation, my high tower, my refuge and my savior; boldly, I praise Him and give God all the glory; Thou saved me from myself. I will call on the Lord, who is worthy to be praised; for no weapon formed against me shall prosper!

The storm has been long, but I'm grateful for the miracles that allowed me to keep moving through and I refuse to let the enemy steal God's glory by preventing my testimony nor will I allow my Joy to be stolen; for our present troubles will soon be over, but Joy from the Lord will last forever!

Following in a "patience of Job" and in my search of knowledge, Job taught me that it is possible to rise above our own limitations by trusting in God, because God is the only one that knows and understand why everything happens and will work situations to the benefit of those who love Him. Like Job, I too recognize now that we do not so much need answers to life's problems as we need God himself and like Job, I love my wife and my wife loves me! In this spiritual war, where the devil lies continuously, I refuse to let the enemy win. Jesus is my Savior and God has been too good to us. I clearly understand now, when we have nothing left but God, God is enough!

Forever being humble, wise and always being mindful of the attacks of the enemy; I give anyone the benefit of doubt and cease being judgmental thus hiding my own faults, but to be revealing in love and thus not blocking the way of my own blessings. God already knew what I would be dealing with in human nature so that's why He sent instructions in the Word! Let those who may be angry or disappointed have patience, an understanding and instead pray for me!

Lord, thank you for a Spirit of Discernment; no bitterness, no malice and no anger here. So shall I forgive, for they know not what they do and be saved from those unknowingly the enemy consumes to trespass against me!!

"It isn't until you come to a spiritual understanding of who you are - not necessarily a religious feeling, but deep down, the spirit within - that you can begin to take control."

Oprah Winfrey

POSTWORD

"I used to get giddy when positive news and updates came down the pike. But now, I don't even get excited. Why? Because I realized that although we are finally here that means that the time has come for us to be smart and strong and unwavering."

"There is so much to do and we've gone through our own personal hell and back to get to this moment. Think about how much you've learned in this process. Think about how your perception has changed in this process. Think about how patient and focused we've been. And we each had outside influences that sought to remove us from this quest. But here we are poised to do great things. Is that not a blessing or what?"

"I am way better than I was when we started this journey. You'll see."

Kemic Smothers, Esq.
VP-Nolatown

"Change does not roll in on the wheels of inevitability, but comes through continuous struggle. And so we must straighten our backs and work for our freedom. A man can't ride you unless your back is bent."

Martin Luther King, Jr.

Appendix: Greatest & Favorites

- ➢ **Greatest Love:** Erica, Kherron and Glenn Jr.
- ➢ **Greatest Fear:** GOD
- ➢ **Greatest Savior:** Jesus Christ
- ➢ **My Heroes:** Roland & Evelyn Broom
- ➢ **Favorite Church:** Berean Christian Church
- ➢ **Favorite Scripture:** Psalm 121
- ➢ **Greatest Advice via Prophecy:** Pursue, Overtake and Conquer
- ➢ **Greatest Moment:** Witnessing births of Kherron and Glenn Jr.
- ➢ **Favorite Drinks:** Coffee with Irish Cream & Sweet Tea
- ➢ **Favorite Balladeer:** Luther Vandross
- ➢ **Favorite Diva:** Whitney Houston
- ➢ **Favorite Singer:** Rachelle Farrell
- ➢ **Favorite Gospel Singer:** Yolanda Adams
- ➢ **Favorite Gospel Family:** The Winans (All of them)
- ➢ **Favorite Music:** R&B, Old School and every now and then a mix of some Hip Hop
- ➢ **Greatest Music Inspiration:** Stevie Wonder
- ➢ **Favorite Movies:** The Shawshank Redemption & Die Hard
- ➢ **Favorite Actor & Actress:** Denzel Washington & Angelina Jolie
- ➢ **Favorite Rapper to Actor/Actress:** Will Smith & Queen Latifah
- ➢ **Favorite Comedian:** Richard Pryor
- ➢ **Favorite All Around Male & Female Entertainer:** Jamie Foxx & Beyonce
- ➢ **Favorite American Idol:** Fantasia
- ➢ **Favorite American Idol that didn't win:** Jennifer Hudson
- ➢ **Favorite Sunday's Best:** Le'Andria Johnson
- ➢ **Favorite Sunday's Best that didn't win:** Jessica Reedy
- ➢ **Favorite Soda:** Coca Cola (Classic)
- ➢ **Favorite Beer:** Heineken
- ➢ **Favorite President & First Lady:** Barrack & Michelle Obama
- ➢ **Favorite Former President & Former First Lady:** Bill & Hillary Clinton
- ➢ **Favorite Politically Correct View:** Do right by the People & the People will do right by you
- ➢ **Favorite TV Talk Show Host:** Oprah
- ➢ **Favorite Hometown Inspiration:** Tyler Perry
- ➢ **Favorite Football Team:** New Orleans Saints (2010 Super Bowl Champs)
- ➢ **Favorite QB:** Drew Brees
- ➢ **Favorite Rivalry & The Team I Love to Hate:** Atlanta Falcons along with their Dirty Birds
- ➢ **Favorite Basketball Team:** New Orleans (Hornets) Pelicans
- ➢ **Favorite Baseball Team:** Atlanta Braves
- ➢ **Greatest Boxer:** Muhammad Ali
- ➢ **Favorite News Anchors:** Rachel Maddow, Keith Olbermann & Lawrence O'Donnell
- ➢ **Favorite Radio/Talk Show Host:** Steve Harvey & Al Sharpton
- ➢ **Greatest Role:** Entrepreneur (Planning & Development)
- ➢ **Favorite Cities:** New Orleans & Atlanta
- ➢ **Favorite Online Computer Game:** Generals: Command & Conqueror (Therapy)
- ➢ **Favorite Foods:** Gumbo and Red Beans & Rice with Fried Chicken & Potato Salad
- ➢ **Favorite Pets (Breed):** Sweetpea & TeddyB (Schnauzers)
- ➢ **Favorite Quotes:** "It's Nice to Be Nice" and of course, "You Got to Believe"
- ➢ **Favorite Bizness Quote:** "Rather have 5% of something, then a 100% of nothing"
- ➢ **Favorite Bizness Risk Quote:** "Can't steal second base and keep one foot on first"
- ➢ **Favorite Chant:** Who Dat Baby!
- ➢ **Favorite Nicknames:** Big Daddy & BigEasy Geezy
- ➢ **Most Important:** Family and Friends

"An Entrepreneur is what you're called when you don't have a job."

Ted Turner

EntrepreNegro

"EntrepreNegro," which I perceive as a business condition many of us brothers find ourselves in where we are sitting on million dollar opportunities, but don't have the resources or the access to the resources to stand up and take advantage of the opportunity. It always seems that the brothers with the plan have no resources and the brothers with the resources have no plan. I know now and realize that it's something divine and faith that puts the two together!

Thank God for patience, guidance, wisdom and understanding. Thank God for not allowing a condition to become a hindrance. Thank God for the support of family and friends. Thank God for the angels sent to fight the demons. Thank God for the favor bestowed upon me. Lastly, thank God for blessing me with an innate ability for process, an understanding of how the numbers work in regards to the process and the ability to translate this information to paper!

Clocked out the pride and clocked in the humility while raising up the praises with testimony in overtime! Most never quite understand the value of planning nor do they acknowledge the effort that goes into it. I'm constantly trying to understand the ones that get the financial breaks along with the trust only to lose their way, thus making it harder for the ones coming behind them trying to do it the right way. I'm mindful of God's timing and know the difference in being patience with a plan that comes with vision, passion and purpose, from foolishness in having no plan and waiting without vision, passion and purpose!

Thank God for a proactive mind instead of reactive one and the vision to see through a situation and therefore, not be stuck in it. I'm truly blessed and highly favored and as I humbly move with the favor I have and spread the Word, I realize sometimes the journey is more important than the destination. For I now understand, through the course of faith and persistence, it takes 30-years of hard work to become an overnight success!

Prophesying with edification in this spiritual warfare, God is my shield, and Jesus is the bridge to my salvation, my high tower, my refuge, my savior; and has been so good to me. Therefore, I've decided to humbly use my life in a way that makes God's heart rejoice and I won't allow anyone or anything to steal my Joy or knock me off the path that God has laid before me! The business plan of my life is complete and I have a roadmap for the world. I understand it now, the devil may be the CEO of the world, but God is the Chairman of the Board and Jesus has successfully overcome the world!

At the end of the day, I recognize that helping people help themselves is the toughest business to be in, but Jesus did it! I've learned to deal with the things I can control and not waste time on things I cannot. In a place where my value is perceived as less, I'll continue to work twice as hard; I'll continue to teach my children to love, not to hate and to recognize the enemy by the content of their character, not by the color of their skin. I'll continue to show them that a plan, patience, humility, persistence and faith are the ingredients for success. I'll continue to empower others and I'll continue to build my value before God whose perception is the only one that I'm truly concerned about!!

Glenn A. Broom

"I have managed to overcome poverty, limited education, segregation and discrimination to become a contributor to society with some national recognition. What I did any man can do – if he has willpower, determination and a plan; so how does a poor man become a businessman? By accumulating money and keeping his eyes open for the main chance."

A.G. Gaston

Goals & Aspirations Timeline:
Buffett vs. Broom

Warren Buffett

1930	Born August 30 to parents US Congressman Howard & Leila Buffett.
1951	Earned Master of Science in Economics from Columbia University.
1952	Married Susan Thompson at Dundee Presbyterian Church (until her death in 2004).
1956	Started Buffett Partnership, Ltd., an investment partnership in Omaha.
1962	Millionaire @ 32 years old.
1970	Acquired and CEO of Berkshire Hathaway @ 40 years old.
5/29/1990	Berkshire Hathaway begins selling Class A shares @ $7,175 a share.
1990	Billionaire and philanthropist @ 60 years old.
2002	11 billion worth of contracts to deliver USD against other currencies for a total gain of 2 billion.
2006	Buffett announced to give away 80% of his total fortune to five foundations. Married Astrid Menks.
2008	Forbes announces Warren Buffett as the richest man in the world.
Quote	"Wall Street is the only place that people ride in a Rolls Royce to get advice from those who take the subway."

Glenn A. Broom

1962	Born June 27 to parents Entrepreneur Roland & Evelyn Broom.
1974	Officially started working in the family business taking over the job of my brother that was passed on to me after being groomed that began at the age of 6.
1988	Married Erica Scipio at Union Bethel AME Church.
1994	Started my first official business and company, Adaptive Medical Supply, LLC.
2001	Started and organized Nolatown.
2003	Moved/commuted back and forth between New Orleans and Atlanta in a dual-residency/business type capacity, while partnered in a pharmacy business in GA and to redevelop my building in Treme.
2004	Nolatown partnership formed w/Rickey Spearman and Kemic Smothers, Esq.
2005	Consulting small businesses in New Orleans and Atlanta. Partnered with Reuben Detiege and wrote grant to Mayor's Office of Economic Development to create and start Virtual Office Suites & Entrepreneurial Center. Nolatown had a deal on the table to purchase downtown Historic Joy Theater. Hurricane Katrina hit New Orleans! Lost office and two years of work in one day with my building in Treme. Nolatown partnered with California developer to reestablish itself back into New Orleans after storm and became liaison for proposed real estate development on a 20 acre site bounded by Lakefront Drive and Leroy Johnson Drive located behind the FBI HQ on the Lakefront. All of the land at the time was owned by the Orleans Levee Board and would have to be leased from the board. Deal fell through when through a legislation change; the State took over the proposed property.
2006	Lincoln Beach introduced to Nolatown as possible site for development.
2007	Spiritual transformation & totally surrendered to God. Received Lincoln Beach prophecy.
2008	Nolatown goes from liaison to lead developer on the Lincoln Beach project.
2009	For the die-hard Saints' fan that I am, who actually picked the Saints to go all the way, when we beat Minnesota in playoffs, for many of us that was our Super Bowl. Nevertheless, this team of destiny took it to the next level and actually wiped out 40-years of despair and disappointment becoming 2010 Super Bowl Champs and the joy of watching it happen in Atlanta in a den full of Dirty Birds, priceless.
2011	My testimony following incident involving Glenn Jr. On September, 13_my hero, my dad passed away.
2014	Published first book, Journey Through A Living Testimony officially as a published Author. Nolatown's Lincoln Beach project groundbreaking.
2015	Millionaire @ 53 years old. Publish second book, You Got To Believe.
2025	Nolatown is a billion dollar corporation.
2026	Billionaire and philanthropist @ 64 years old.
Quote	"Never conclude until you know all the facts or close the book before reading the entire story because it's not only bittersweet, but hard to understand you with your foot in your mouth and of course, You Got To Believe!"

"Its fine to celebrate success, but it is more important to heed the lessons of failure."

Bill Gates

"We Are Family"

"I got my mother, my brother and my sisters with me!"

"I would unite with anybody to do right and

with nobody to do wrong."

Frederick Douglas

Meet TeddyB!

"Who Dat say Who Dat when I say Who Dat"

&

"It's Nice to be Nice"

Roland & Evelyn Broom

R.I.P SweetPea!

"One day it will all come together and everything will make sense. You will see God's amazing plan taking you places you've never dreamed of."

Joel Osteen

My Wall

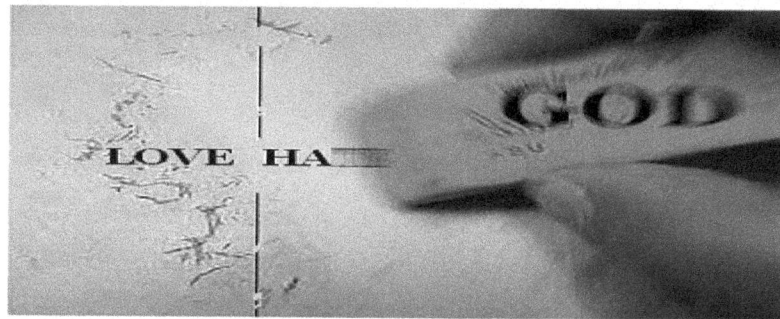

"It's a thin line between love and hate, but when God is the eraser, love triumphs!"
Glenn A. Broom

"I just wanna thank you, forever, and ever, and ever... For all... you've done, done for me...." "Blessings and honor... and glory..., they all belong to you..." "Thank you Jesus for blessing... me"

Legacy

What would my legacy be and what would I want people to remember about me? I'm a humble God fearing man who loves Jesus, have deep love and adoration for my family and friends; love to have a good time, have a mind for business and empowering others; that I'm rejoicing with a purpose in this life that the Lord has made and I'm grateful to be in it; that life experiences made me tough, not hard and it's nice to be nice; that I'm a doer and I don't quit!!

Glenn A. Broom